Prestel

MAX E

Prestel

Munich · Berlin · London · New York

MUSEUM BRÜHL

Frontispiece
Max Ernst Museum
Dance hall with *Capricorn*
group of figures, 2005
Bronze
Permanent loan, Deutsche Bank

© Prestel Verlag, Munich · Berlin · London · New York, 2005
© for the works of Max Ernst VG Bildkunst, Bonn, 2005

Concept and editing by Susanne Blöcker
Published by Max Ernst Museum Brühl
Cover photo by Manfred J. Junggeburth
Frontispiece by Harald Blondiau

The Library of Congress Cataloguing-in-Publication data is
available; British Library Cataloguing-in-Publication Data:
a catalogue record for this book is available from the British
Library; Deutsche Bibliothek holds a record of this publication
in the Deutsche Nationalbibliografie; detailed bibliographical
data can be found under: http://dnb.ddb.de

Prestel Verlag	Prestel Publishing Ltd.	Prestel Publishing
Königinstrasse 9	4 Bloomsbury Place	900 Broadway, Suite 603
80539 Munich	London WC1A 2QA	New York, NY 10003
Tel. +49 (89) 38 17 09-0	Tel. +44 (20) 73 23-5004	Tel. +1 (212) 995-2720
Fax +49 (89) 38 17 09-35	Fax +44 (20) 76 36-8004	Fax +1 (212) 995-2733

www.prestel.com

Translated from the German by Paul Aston
Copy-edited by Danko Szabó, Munich
Layout and production by a.visus, Michael Hempel, Munich
Origination by Reproline mediateam, Munich
Printing and binding by Print Consult, Munich

Printed in Germany on acid-free paper

ISBN 3-7913-3417-4 (English edition)
ISBN 3-7913-3415-8 (French edition)
ISBN 3-7913-3416-6 (German edition)

FOREWORD	6
THE ARCHITECTURE OF THE MUSEUM	10
THE EARLY WORK OF MAX ERNST 1891–1914	17
MAX ERNST IN COLOGNE 1918–1922	25
MAX ERNST IN FRANCE 1922–1941	30
THE YEARS IN THE USA 1941–1949	38
D-PAINTINGS Landscapes of Love	45
MAX ERNST RETURNS TO FRANCE 1949–1976	52
WORKING METHODS AND TECHNIQUES	62
BIOGRAPHY	70
Bibliography	76
Information about the Museum	78
Photo Credits	80

FOREWORD

Werner Spies

Max Ernst has now a wonderful museum all to himself – you could call the building itself eloquent architecture, because it is a happy combination of the 19th century and the days when Ernst himself was alive and working. The end result was an amalgam that did not do away with the old building that Max Ernst went in and out of in his youth, but refashioned it. In that respect, it echoes Ernst's own collage procedures. As a technical and intellectual process, collage was a key feature throughout his works. He started out as an artist working from a confusing medley of reproductions. The objects and information that he came across in late 19th-century publications furnished material for him to recycle, and he served it up in wonderful collages, pictures, books, drawings, sculptures and writings. He started experimenting very early on. From 1919, he felt his way forward with a series of venturesome works into a realm that he described as "beyond painting".

The core of the Brühl collection is an extensive corpus of wonderful sculptures from the artist's estate. Besides these, there are a number of pictures, hundreds of drawings, and books, photographs and documents. They trace the career of one of the greatest spirits of the 20th century. The various phases of his life – his time in the Rhineland, his triumphal success in Paris, the years in the US and his return to Europe in the 1950s – are illustrated with specific

Lord Snowdon
Max Ernst working on a plaster model of *Capricorn*
Huismes, November 1963

examples. Max Ernst was someone for whom even the most trivial observations from life often constituted the starting point for a disconcerting change of tack. Viewers of his labyrinthine pictorial world generally find themselves at a loss to name another artist who is so chronically difficult to pigeonhole easily and pithily. His inventiveness in handling pictorial techniques and the well of inspiration, the discontinuities that crop up between the numerous phases of his work, the revolving subject matter – every aspect throws all the labels up in the air again.

Max Ernst himself puts his finger on a reason behind this muddle – perhaps even the motivation for it: *A painter may know what he doesn't want. But woe betide him if he wants to know what he does want! Painters are lost if they find who they really are.* That he successfully failed to discover who he really was, Max Ernst considers as his "sole" merit.

Art critics first polarised Picasso and Max Ernst as complementary but opposing ends of the 20th-century artistic spectrum in the 1930s. Attempts were made to circumscribe and rationalise Picasso's stupendous and disturbing range of forms that can be described as Protean, and the same word can be applied to Max Ernst, though for different reasons. A first glance reveals that with Ernst, the only certainty is that the message is unclear and the denial of interpretation deliberate. The constant leap from microscopic formats full of pictorial wit and private introspection to shatteringly monumental visions comes as a shock. You feel that it is not just a matter of private mythologies and angst-ridden dreams – behind them lie collective experiences which Ernst translated into pictures. They are pictures that patently represent what 20th-century history painting might come up with if it were condensed into a system of signals of angst and destruction. Alongside these there is a constant supply of more harmonious, brighter works in which sorrow and horror make way for a virtual cosmic cheerfulness. The two are closely associated in this pictorial world, so intimately in contact with each other that day could become night, cheerfulness paralysis at any moment.

FOREWORD

Nightmares and liberation – that is what Ernst offers us in his oeuvre, which spanned a period of almost 70 years.

To quote his own words: *Painting operates on two different and yet complementary levels. It furnishes aggression and uplift.*

It is high time that the present day recognised itself in this "miraculously inspirited spirit", as Andre Breton put it, and rediscovered an exemplary work and life. The museum in Brühl aims to foster this vital, ongoing process of rediscovery.

Max Ernst Museum, 2004
Comesstraße
Photo: Rainer Mader

Comesstraße 42 / Max-Ernst-Allee 1
50321 Brühl (Rheinland)
Tel   02234 9921 – 555
Fax   02234 9921 – 300
E-Mail: info@maxernstmuseum.de
Homepage: www.maxernstmuseum.lvr.de

Öffnungszeiten

Dienstag – Sonntag: 11 – 18 Uhr
1. Donnerstag im Monat: 11 – 21 Uhr

Geschlossen: jeden Montag, 1.1., Weiberfastnacht, Karnevalssonntag, Rosenmontag, Karfreitag, Ostermontag, 1.5., Pfingstmontag, 24., 25., 31.12.

gefördert durch:

Max Ernst Museum Brühl

```
        Erwachs. Einzeleintritt
               40114
  1    x         5,00              5,00

  Gesamtsumme    EUR               5,00

            keine Mehrwertsteuer

  Gegeben BAR   EUR                5,00
  Zurück        EUR                0,00
            Ihr Besuch freut uns!

Bon 00-00192401 05.04.11 11:01:21
```

*where years ago a house stood
there a house is now growing*
Max Ernst

THE ARCHITECTURE OF THE MUSEUM

Andreas Rossmann

Old and new form an integral unity in the Max Ernst Museum without superficially seeming reconciled. Stone and glass, pitched roof and flat roof are discreetly juxtaposed without being in direct contact. Indeed, each 'half' emphasises its individuality – yet they are so interrelated and linked underground that functionally they complement each other. The one literally 'stands by' the other, in a mutually supportive relationship.

The design was put out to competition in 2001, and 841 applications were received from the whole of Europe, of which 36 pre-qualified. The winning submission by Cologne-based architect Thomas van den Valentyn proposed taking the building back to its original condition, on the principle of prudence and respect. The character of the three-block Neoclassical building, which is a small-scale echo of the nearby Augustusburg Palace (Schloss Augustusburg), was thereby preserved, and cleared of a clutter of disfiguring later extensions and insertions. The original ground plan was U-shaped. Valentyn and Seyed Mohammad Oreyzi, who formed a partnership for the job, left its basic fabric unimpaired, and even the new pavilion – a steel and glass structure placed carefully but with great aplomb centrally to the side wings – preserves a discreet distance.

The old building has had a chequered history. It was built in 1844 at the same time as the Cologne-Bonn railway, and

up to World War I the 'Brühl Pavilion' was a popular venue for outings and entertainment. As an older teenager, Max Ernst himself shook a leg on the dance floor here. The building subsequently underwent several changes of use – in 1919, the Salvator nuns turned it into a children's home, which the Catholic Caritas charity expanded into a home for children and mothers in 1930. Partially destroyed in World War II, the building housed sick infants from 1946, until in 1953 the Dienerinnen des Herzens Jesu nuns took it over for the Benediktus Old People's Home. In 1990, facing a shortage of recruits, the order sold the building – which had been listed in 1984 – to the town of Brühl. Thereafter it provided accommodation for asylum-seekers until in 2001 the municipality opted for the museum scheme and restoration.

The platform on which the new pavilion stands is slightly higher than the prevailing levels, and the building seems to positively float in the landscape. Its dimensions and articulation pick up the rhythm of bays in the old building's façade, and the width of the polished stone strips that mark them out (23.6 cm / 9 1/4") correspond exactly to the thickness of the walls. An area of serpentino, a grey-green granite from Sondrio in Northern Italy, creates a public stage running

Max Ernst Museum, 2005
Front view in the evening
Photo: Rainer Mader

THE ARCHITECTURE OF THE MUSEUM

from the forecourt to the lobby. Outside, visitors are greeted by a sculptural group, the *Corps enseignant pour une école de tueurs* (1967, *Teaching Staff for a School of Killers*) with the three figures *Big Brother*, *Séraphine Cherubin* and *Séraphin le Néophyte*.

Conceptually, the design of the pavilion evolved from an examination of the situation and how it could function as a backdrop for the museum programme. Its sculptural structure is the result of a daylight study, and functions as a kind of diffuser distributing light into the lower rooms and conditioning it for the works of art. The glass façades are partly covered with dot screens to filter out ultraviolet light without impairing sightlines between the interior and exterior. The double-layer steel structure and construction on several levels reflect the function of the pavilion as an optical instrument. The effect of this is both monolithic and filigree. The transparent, closed and opaque walls positively give the pavilion the appearance of growing out of the ground while admitting daylight via slits in the floor into the room below where temporary exhibitions are put on.

Max Ernst
Séraphin le Néophyte, 1967
Bronze, Permanent loan,
Kreissparkasse Köln
Photo: Rainer Mader

Max Ernst Museum, 2004
Foyer
Photo: Rainer Mader

Max Ernst Museum, 2004
Area for temporary exhibitions
Photo: Rainer Mader

From the entrance on the western side, the visitor passes the museum shop and ticket office and goes down into a subterranean, *subconscious* world via steel stairs or a perforated-plate lift. On the first below-ground level is a small foyer with entrances to the old building, whose side buildings are linked via a gallery. The open staircase leads to the room for temporary exhibitions and the 340-seat Events Room, which is laid with oak parquet and wood panelling and gets by without additional acoustic aids, as they were built into the structure, for example, the pleated walls and fanned ceiling. With an area of 500 m²/ 5,370 sq.ft. and a height of 5.5 m/18 ft., the room for temporary exhibitions is of a size that disregards the scale of the old building, yet it seems neither overlarge nor like a cellar.

THE ARCHITECTURE OF THE MUSEUM

The reason for this is the link with the outer world. A surprising amount of natural daylight comes in, dividing up the room in various ways. The atmosphere is that of a workshop, with cream-coloured flooring of Crailsheim muschelkalk and walls which, where they continue into the pavilion above, are painted white or are otherwise in exposed concrete, create surreal impressions. The light well by the end wall attracts the eye towards the brighter area.

The old building, which with its loggias and façade articulation has regained a degree of grandeur and dignity, is reserved for Max Ernst. All the layers of paint were removed from the façade and the fabric repainted in the original light grey. The stucco and damaged masonry were repaired and improved and the windows reinstated on the original pattern. The upper floor is opened up via the historic steps on the north side and new mirror-image steps on the south side, while in the wings the historic gallery walls have been retained, the surfaces being covered by several layers of white stucco. The main block provides floor space of 930 m² / 10,000 sq.ft. for the permanent display. To some

Max Ernst Museum, 2004
Gallery
Photo: Rainer Mader

Max Ernst Museum, 2004
Dance hall
Photo: Rainer Mader

extent reorganised, the purist interior constitutes a succession of cabinet rooms whose oiled white oak parquet radiates a distinguished elegance. The administration is on the ground floor of the south wing, while the catering area is in the north wing.

In the way they have simplified the complexity and unobtrusively attuned the materials to each other, Seyed Mohammad Oreyzi and project manager Gloria Amling have retained the special character of the place and created a building for contemplation that is deliberately subordinated to the service of art.

Thus Max Ernst has returned to his former dance hall, restored to its historic state with its graceful cast-iron columns, to get the world dancing with his puzzle pictures and dream landscapes, his wonderland logic and sceptical dissection of reality. Quite unexpectedly, Ernst's prophetic words in the last two lines of his fabulous narrative poem 'Bird Couple' (1953) apply to this place:

where years ago a house stood
there a house is now growing

Chaos in my head. In painting as well.
Max Ernst

THE EARLY WORK OF MAX ERNST 1891–1914

Susanne Blöcker

*At 9 45 am on 2 April 1891,
Max Ernst had his first contact
with the tangible world
when he hatched out of the egg.*
Max Ernst, Things from Max Ernst's Youth, Told by Himself

Waiting for him at 21 Schloss Strasse in Brühl were his father, Philipp Ernst, a strict deaf-mute teacher at the school there, and his wife, Luise, née Kopp, who, according to Max Ernst, was full of fun and stories.

The key influences on family life were the Catholic faith, paternal authority and the conservative ideals of the late Victorian era, which Philipp Ernst rendered into pictorial form.

Unknown
Haus Erven, at 21 Schlossstraße in Brühl, where Max Ernst was born, c. 1910
Private collection

Unknown
Max Ernst's parents: Luise Ernst, née Kopp, and Philipp Ernst, c. 1886
Private collection

Max Ernst
Study of Brühl Park
c. 1909
Watercolour

THE EARLY WORK 1891–1914

Unknown
Max Ernst as a painter
Brühl, 1909
Vintage, silver bromide print

With meticulous precision and craft skill, he copied the great masters of the past, orienting his approach – like many historicist painters – to that of Raphael.

And his eldest son, Max, was always there, appearing as a figure drawn by his father (for example, in *Portrait of Max Ernst, Aged 5, as the Child Jesus,* 1896) or strolling with him, even as a three-year old, through the nearby palace park or local woods. Philipp Ernst was young Max's first model to look up to, both in drawing and his love of nature. Sometimes his father would record a scene in a magic wood (*Solitude,* 1894) in which every beech leaf vibrated with a life of its own, or he and his son would collect plants, stones or beetles. This is where the *Histoire Naturelle* began, and this was the fertile soil in Brühl for the fantastic, surreal landscapes of Max Ernst. It all began at Augustusburg Palace, in the avenues of Brühl Park. This is where the young Max found subjects for his first pictures and sketched them in watercolours.

He was 18, *and his eyes drink in everything that enters his vision.* Max Ernst *Wahrheitgewebe*

This included the philosophical writings of Max Stirner, the Romantics, fairy stories and legends, and the art in Rhineland museums. The latter ranged from old masters at the Wallraf-Richartz Museum in Cologne, whose imaginary worlds fascinated him, to progressive exhibitions such as the *Sonderbund* in Cologne in 1912, which introduced him to the contemporary art scene. As a young artist, he was particularly struck by the intense colours of Van Gogh, as is evident from his *Self-Portrait* of 1909. Examining himself in the mirror, he sought for an identity in the clarity and intensity of his colours. It was a quest Ernst continued at the university in Bonn. Enrolling in April 1910, he dabbled in philology, art history, German language and literature, Romance languages and literature, philosophy, archaeology, law, psychiatry and psychology. He threshed around, looking this way and that with "chaos in his head" (see *Wahrheitgewebe*). For financial reasons he was still living at home, commuting from Brühl to Bonn, so that Brühl railway station became an important point of reference for him. Ever since his childhood, it had been a lure for him.

Max Ernst
Self-Portrait, 1909
Oil on card

THE EARLY WORK 1891–1914

That was where the wide world began, and that is where he took off to when the strictness of the parental home became too much. It is therefore no surprise that he recorded the *Railway Underpass in Comesstrasse* in an oil painting in 1912, again in a Van Gogh style, the model being the latter's *Railway Bridge over Avenue Montmajour* of 1888. The scene displays a similar vigour of brush stroke, but unlike the Dutch master, Ernst's gaze did not plunge into the depths of the underpass but went straight up to the telegraph wires.

Max Ernst
Railway Underpass in Comesstraße, 1912
Oil on card

They move heavily if you watch them through the compartment window of moving trains, and suddenly stop moving when the train stops. Max Ernst *Wahrheitgewebe*

    Max Ernst himself was constantly on the move during this period. From his 19th to his 23rd year he took on board everything that painting had to offer. In his early works he made use of the avantgarde art that came his way. Whether he was in Bonn, Düsseldorf or Cologne, his works positively reflected the supercharged atmosphere of the art scene in the pre-war years, which exploded into expression and passion and constantly changed – in the juxtaposition of ideas as much as in the people involved. Even during his years in Bonn, he had become part of the art scene. That was when he made the acquaintance of Hans Arp in 1914, who remained a friend for over half a century. There, too, he came across his most important mentor and fatherly friend, the Bonn painter August Macke, who was already well-known. Macke had been easing him into art and the Rhineland group of Expressionist artists since 1911. Though only a few years older than Max Ernst, he was well-travelled and experienced, and so was able to encourage the Bonn student and give him security. That was how Ernst decided to become a painter.

    At the *Sonderbund* exhibition in Cologne in 1912, Max Ernst became familiar with the violent coloration of the Fauvists and

Max Ernst
Still Life in the Sitting Room, 1912
Oil on card

Max Ernst
Paris Boulevard, 1913
Oil on paper

THE EARLY WORK 1891–1914

Max Ernst
Lady in Green Dress, c. 1913
Pencil, Indian ink and watercolour on paper

the crystalline, exploded motifs of the Cubist world, along with the abstract colour harmonies of the expressive Blauer Reiter painters from Munich and the vivid works and reduced shapes of the *Brücke* painters. Impressed by the Fauvists, Ernst painted shortly afterwards the almost abstract-looking *Still Life in the Sitting Room*, which is dominated by ornamental, gleaming colour surfaces and shapes, whose fluidity is held in check only by black outlines. A trip to Paris by the Art History Institute of Bonn in summer 1913 provided him with his first direct contact with the artists' mecca. Once there, he was desperate to record his impressions, for example, the *Paris Boulevard* or the close-up of an elegant *Lady in a Green Dress*. In a frenzy of drawing, he put down on paper everything he saw, in the company of his fellow student and future wife, Luise Straus. Once they were back home, the pair of them described their heady experiences in Paris to August Macke and his Expressionist friends, prompting the poet Karl Otten to say later: *We sat beneath the foliage in the garden by the Rhine and saw Cologne and Bonn as suburbs of Paris, Vienna and Rome.*

The vigour of their style and rejection of late 19th-century pathetic formulae made the group – which now included the young Max Ernst – the hub of Rhineland Expressionism. But this inspirational artistic community was not destined to last long. Arp was the first to realise it in 1914, while Max Ernst and Franz Henseler saw it in spiritualist séances – World War I would bring death. It took their lodestar August Macke from them and destroyed the group.

Max Ernst died on 1 August 1914.
He returned to life on 11 November 1918
as a young man who wanted to become
a magician and discover the myth of his day.
Max Ernst *Einiges aus Max Ernsts Jugend von ihm selbst erzählt*

He found it in Dadaism and, later, in Surrealism.

Dada was a bomb
Max Ernst

MAX ERNST IN COLOGNE 1918–1922

Anne Ganteführer-Trier

After World War I broke out, Dada centres were formed in quick succession between 1915 and 1917 in Zurich, New York, Barcelona, Paris and Berlin. The early Dada movement was a horrified response to the brutality of war.
We none of us had the taste for the courage you need to get yourself shot dead for the ideas of a nation, which is at best a syndicate of fur dealers and leather racketeers, in the worst case a bunch of psychopaths who set off in the German "fatherland" with a volume of Goethe in their knapsacks to run Frenchmen and Russians through with their bayonets. Richard Huelsenbeck, quoted from Elger/Grosenick, p. 8

Asked as to what the content of Dada was, Zurich-based Dadaist Richard Huelsenbeck replied:
Asking what Dada is, is unDada. You can't understand Dada, you have to experience it. Dada is direct and self-explanatory. Dada makes a kind of anti-cultural propaganda out of honesty, revulsion and profound disgust at the affectation of superiority by the intellectually certified bourgeoisie.
quoted from Werner Lippert, in: exhib. cat. *Vom Dadamax*, p. 34)

Even during his military service, Max Ernst kept up close contacts with various Dada activists. Shortly before the outbreak of war, he had made the acquaintance of Hans Arp in 1914, during a tour of the Werkbund exhibition in Cologne. Leave from the front in 1916, which he used to travel to Berlin, led him to George Grosz and Wieland Herzfelde, who

soon after caused a stir in Berlin with their Dada projects. By April 1917, Max Ernst himself was represented in the second Storm exhibition at the Galerie Dada in Zurich.

At the end of 1918, Max Ernst was demobbed and returned to Cologne. There he ('Minimax-Dadamax'), Johannes Theodor Baargeld (a.k.a. Alfred Ferdinand Grünwald) and Hans Arp formed the Cologne Dada group, which put on its first exhibition at the Kunstverein in Cologne the same year. In the shadow of Cologne Cathedral, Max Ernst, Theodor Baargeld and their friends provoked their first Dadaist sensation. Less for political reasons than by way of cocking a snook at existing trends in art, particularly Expressionism, they exhibited drawings by children and dilettantes. Exhibit no. 60, a *Piano Hammer made by Mand*, was in Max Ernst's view a perfect piece of sculpture: *People love everyone's Expressionists, but throw up their hands in horror at the sight of inspired drawings of urinals. The most perfect sculpture is a piano hammer. dada.* Max Ernst *Über Cézanne*, 1919

The exhibition also contained eight original lithos by Ernst called *Fiat modes, pereat ars* (Let Fashion Flourish, Art Expire), which he dedicated to Giorgio de Chirico.

An advert in *Die Schammade*, a periodical published by Ernst and Baargeld, announced in 1920: *Fiat modes (pereat ars), eight signed original lithographs (FIAT MODES) chicdada*

Unknown
Hans Arp and Max Ernst
Cologne, c. 1920
Rolandseck, Stiftung Hans Arp
und Sophie Taeuber-Arp

Max Ernst
Fiat modes, pereat ars, 1919
One of eight lithographs

MAX ERNST. ... the pictures were drawn for the City of Cologne. This is the first case we know of in which a city administration has commissioned a dadaist work of art. Cologne is on the march.

Max Ernst described the city's assumption of the costs as "unemployment benefit".

The *Fiat Modes* drawings manifest a typically Cubist idiom assembling several different perspectives into a single picture, but there are also echoes of the stiff figures of de Chirico's Pittura Metafisica. (Ernst had come across and admired these only shortly before.) But the series only hints at the diversity and extent of Max Ernst's Dada works during this period. Ernst also did mixed-genre collages and assem-

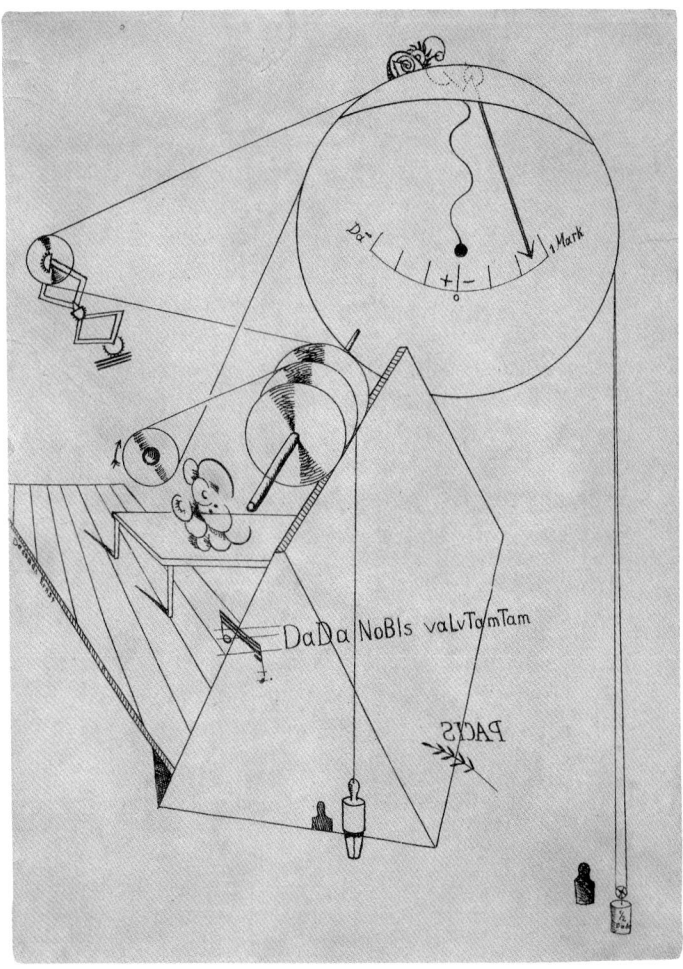

blages made up of photos, drawings, overpaintings and typographical elements.

The Cologne Dadaists were soon publishing periodicals to voice their protest in art. The first issue of *Bulletin D* appeared in 1919, only to be impounded because of a socialist-minded essay by Otto Freundlich. *Ventilator*, published in the same year, was immediately banned by the British occupation force.

In 1920, a second Dada exhibition was put on in the rented light well of Winter's Brewery in Cologne. Beside the three Cologne-based protagonists Hans Arp, J. T. Baargeld and Max Ernst, Francis Picabia from Paris also took part. According to eye witnesses, the exhibition was accused of 'obscenity' because access was possible only via the bar urinal and it was assumed to be a brothel for homosexuals. The poster DADA WINS, announcing the "reopening of the exhibition closed by the police", documents the temporary closure of the exhibition.

Likewise in 1920, Max Ernst also made contact with the legendary art dealer Johanna Ey, whose gallery was called Neue Kunst Frau Ey (New Art Mrs. Ey) even then. In November 1921, she put on the first exhibition of Dada works by Max Ernst. Looking back, Gert Wollheim, a close associate of Johanna Ey's, reported: *There was a "plastoma" in the exhibition called The "Bone Mills of the Thunderless Hairdressers", in the style of "Miller's Wire Springtime" by Kurt Schwitters, which we had already exhibited.* quoted from Barth, p.34

Meantime, Max Ernst published his much-quoted Dadaist biography in the second issue of the *Junges Rheinland* periodical: *Born in Brühl in 1891...currently lives in Cologne, now...a painter in his early 30s, less from a love of art than from laziness and ancient tradition....Since then, he likes playing with the filiform protuberances of the coast region and foothills. Woman for him is a roll filled with white marble.*

The Dada group in Cologne began to break up already in 1920, when it lost a vital pacemaker in Hans Arp, who left the city. One year later, with the assistance of André Breton, Max Ernst put on his first exhibition in Paris. The feedback from this prompted him to move there in 1922 and take up

IN COLOGNE 1918–1922

Surrealism. However, the contact with Johanna Ey in Düsseldorf remained intact while he was in Paris. *At that time, Max Ernst often came to Mother Ey from Paris, bringing with him as many works as he could carry. Some of these were left with her on consignment, while others were bought outright by Mother Ey, Gert Wollheim or exhibition visitors, so that after a few days he could set off for Paris again. He was quiet, reserved and dressed like a gentleman* (quoted from Barth, p. 42), recalled Trude Brück.

Simone Breton
Jacques Rigaut, Tristan Tzara and André Breton, Paris, 1920
seated in front of Max Ernst's photo collage *Der Schwan ist sehr friedlich / The Swan is Very Peaceful*

Max Ernst
Conseils d'ami, wall frieze
from the house of Paul Eluard
in Eaubonne, 1923
Oil on plaster, transferred to canvas
Permanent loan, Kreissparkasse Köln

MAX ERNST IN FRANCE 1922–1941

Katja Tallner

> *It [frottage] excludes all conscious
> mental control (reason, taste, morality)
> and limits in the extreme
> the active input of the person
> hitherto called the 'author'
> of the work.*
>
> Max Ernst *Beyond Painting*

In 1922, Max Ernst finally turned his back on Germany. For the time being, he lived with the poet Paul Eluard and his wife, Gala, in Saint-Brice-sous-Forêt in the Île de France. Jointly produced books of poems (*Répétitions* and *Les Malheurs des Immortels*) testify to the ties of close friendship between Eluard and Ernst right from their first encounter in Cologne. Ernst used 19th-century wood engravings for the collages published in these volumes, the bits he cut out of them being rearranged into new compositions. This process of linking apparently remote things led to "poetic detonations", according to Max Ernst in *What is Surrealism?* – just like the image that the Surrealists liked to quote of the encounter between a sewing machine and an umbrella on a dissecting table (Lautréamont).

Max Ernst did a number of murals in his host's new house in Eaubonne, an important series of paintings that was only rediscovered by Eluard's daughter Cécile in 1967, who remembered the intense colours and fantastic landscapes in her bedroom as a child.

In 1924, all the talk among the Parisian avantgarde revolved around one topic – André Breton's recently published 'First Manifesto of Surrealism', in which he demanded a "rejection of the dominance of logic, a mental diktat not subject to any control by reason". Thoughts were to be devoid of purpose (automatism) just as they are in dreams and hallucinations, and this was declared to be a major objective of the Surrealists.

A year after the publication of the Surrealist manifesto, Max Ernst made an extraordinary discovery: *One rainy day in an inn on the coast, I was overcome by the visual force and mesmerising effect of thousands of scratch marks on the floorboards. I decided to investigate the symbolism of this compulsive process and did a series of drawings of the floorboards to boost my meditative and hallucinatory capabilities. To do it, I put drawing paper down on the floor randomly and rubbed over it with a pencil lead. When I looked at the drawings this produced … I was surprised at the sudden intensification of my visionary capabilities and the hallucinatory consequence of contradictory pictures that piled up at great speed and with great urgency.*

Max Ernst *Beyond Painting*

Max Ernst's discovery of frottage provided him with a way of working that enabled him to comply with Breton's literarily inspired demand for an equivalent to *écriture automatique* in art. The best examples of the technique are the 34 sheets of the *Histoire Naturelle*, published in 1926. The diversity of texture in the materials involved, for example, wooden planks, leaves and straw, furnished him with numerous real-world associations and interpretations.

Another technique Max Ernst came up with in his quest for new technical tricks that would skip the direct application of paint and so keep him as an artist out of the gestation of the work was grattage. In this, paint is scratched off the canvas so as to reveal the structures of the objects beneath, allowing a variety of interpretations. Two subjects

that were particular favourites of his at this time – woods and birds – frequently recur later as well.

From 1929, he worked at three impressive collage novels containing over 400 works – *La femme 100 têtes* (1929), *Rêve d'une petite fille qui voulut entrer au Carmel* (1930) and *Une semaine de bonté* (1934). His raw material was illustrations taken from light fiction and 19th-century popular science magazines. Ernst no longer composed the pictures just using separate items as he had in earlier works but took over complete scenes, replacing or supplementing individual elements in them himself. In the words of René Crevel, he became a kind of "magician of scarcely perceptible shifts". His interventions produced unreal, absurd-looking situations which often involved hybrid human and animal creatures. As the collages were duplicated by photographic means, no traces of the artistic manipulations can be discerned. The familiar look of the subject matter lends the pictures an initial stylistic unity, but when you take a closer look the scenes are not so cosy after all. The titles of the pictures, inasmuch as the works have any sort of commentary at all, add to your discomfort. The scenes are absurd and intended to leave you flailing around for interpretations, particularly as there is another level of reality that is both disturbing

Max Ernst
L'évadé / Escaped Prisoner,
sheet 30 from *Histoire Naturelle*, 1926
Collotype print from frottage

and fascinating. In *La Femme 100 têtes* (a punning title – 'The Woman with 100 Heads' but as spoken also meaning 'The Woman with-out a Head') we encounter for the first time a 'loplop' figure, whose bird-like features would develop in the following years. In his autobiographical notes, Max Ernst describes this figure as a 'phantom' that was truly devoted to him. Loplop became a figure of identification that presents his artistic discoveries in many works.

Max Ernst spent summer 1935 with Alberto Giacometti in Maloja (Switzerland). The natural curves of the granite pebbles from the moraines of the Forno Glacier fascinated both artists so much that they painted over twenty spherical and oval found objects in free association and scratched

Max Ernst
"…mon âme fut inondée de la rosée céleste…"/"…my soul was flooded with the celestial dawn…", illustration for *Rêve d'une petite fille qui volut entrer au Carmel*, 1929/1930, Wood engraving collage

IN FRANCE 1922–1941

their 'secrets' into them. Three of these unusual stones are in the collection of the Max Ernst Foundation. The works formed the starting point for Max Ernst's subsequent freestanding sculptures, in which he invested his 'Dada experience'. Going on from the readymades of Marcel Duchamps, who took ordinary objects out of the normal contexts and dished them up as works of art, Ernst used ordinary objects such as bottles or flower vases as moulds. Works made by such combinations include *Habakuk*, *Oiseau-tête* and *Oedipus II* – strange and at the same time funny imaginary beings made of plaster, which were later cast in bronze.

Max Ernst
Loplop présente, 1931
Collage and pencil on paper,
motif sprayed with colour
Gift of the Kultur- and Umwelt-
stiftung der Kreissparkasse Köln

Decalcomania was an artistic technique discovered by Oscar Dominguez in 1936, and Ernst made use of it in his paintings as another 'indirect' technique. It was an extra way of avoiding direct brushstrokes. It required a smooth, hard surface, for example, a pane of glass, to press oil paint on to the support. The soft, fluid structures thereby produced Ernst generally interpreted as comical landscapes or rock formations, and he worked them up accordingly with various techniques.

In 1938, when he left the group of Surrealists associated with Breton out of solidarity with Paul Eluard, Max Ernst turned his back on Paris in order to live with British artist Leonora Carrington in Saint-Martin d'Ardèche, north of Avignon. There he provided her dilapidated, vineyard-surrounded cottage with cement reliefs that caused a stir.

However, the idyllic peace in southern France did not last long. In 1939, political reality caught up with them. Two years earlier, his works had been branded as 'degenerate' by the Nazis and confiscated. After the outbreak of World War II, Max Ernst was interned several times as an 'enemy

Max Ernst
Habakuk/Habakkuk, 1934
Bronze, Permanent loan,
Kreissparkasse Köln

Max Ernst
Oiseau-tête/Bird head
1934/1935
Bronze, Permanent loan,
Kreissparkasse Köln

IN FRANCE 1922–1941

alien', for example, in the camp in Les Milles near Aix-en-Provence. In 1941, he succeeded in escaping from France, and with the help of art collector Peggy Guggenheim emigrated via Lisbon to the USA.

Kurt Bingler
Figure from the main group of the cement relief
Saint-Martin d'Ardèche, 1961
Vintage, gelatin silver print

Arnold Newman
Max Ernst, New York, 1942
Later gelatin silver print

Freedom, beloved freedom
Max Ernst *Wahrheitgewebe*

THE YEARS IN THE USA 1941–1949

Verena Schneider

In July 1941, Max Ernst emigrated to New York with art collector Peggy Guggenheim, via Madrid and Lisbon. On their arrival, the couple got married and moved into a house in Beekman Place, near the East River. The 'Guggenheim triplex' soon became a meeting place for both American and European artists.

During this time, many photographer friends took photos of Max Ernst. For example, Arnold Newman shows him sitting in an old-fashioned chair with contemporary paintings in the background. The smoke from the cigarette, in which the silhouette of a bird appears, lends the artist a mysterious otherworldliness, creating the aura of a magician.

Early on during his years in the USA, Max Ernst took part in the spectacular *First Papers of Surrealism* exhibition along with artists such as Robert Motherwell and Yves Tanguy. The exhibition was organised by André Breton and provided with a net of cords by Marcel Duchamp. In 1942 came a presentation in the Wakefield Bookshop in New York. The painting of a *Young Man Fretting While Watching the Flight of a Non-Euclidean Fly* he showed there awoke the interest of fellow painters. In it, Max Ernst used a new technique which he called 'oscillation' and the Americans later called 'dripping'. The technique had already been employed by Francis Picabia in 1917, though it had aroused no interest at the time. It was a technique based on the randomness. Max Ernst suggested:

Tie an empty can to a cord three to six feet long, drill a hole in the bottom and fill the tin with runny paint. Let the tin swing backwards and forwards on the cord over the canvas on the floor while controlling the tin with movements of the hands, arms, shoulders and your whole body. This way you get surprising lines on the canvas. At that point, you can start to think about what you've got. Max Ernst *Écritures*

The technique proved a momentous development. Later, Jackson Pollock took it over and made it famous as 'Action Painting'.

In 1942, Max Ernst became acquainted with American artist Dorothea Tanning, and they went on holiday together to Arizona several times. In the Grand Canyon he recognised a landscape he had earlier painted from imagination in France. His enthusiasm for the region was reinforced by his interest in the culture of the Pueblo Indians who lived there. The Surrealists had focused on Indian art ever since the mid-1920s. In contrast to the German *Brücke* artists,

John D. Schiff
View of the *First Papers of Surrealism* exhibition staged by André Breton, cords by Marcel Duchamp,
New York, October 1942

THE YEARS IN THE USA 1941–1949

it was not formal aspects that attracted their attention but spiritual affinities with the Indians. Max Ernst was particularly drawn by the myths and rites that he got to know when he visited the reservations. A photo by Lee Miller shows him in his house in Sedona with a Hopi mask – an act of self-portraiture as a magician.

The fascination that Indian culture exerted on Max Ernst is to some extent reflected in his work. In his first visit to an Indian reservation he discovered a large number of old

Lee Miller
Max Ernst with a Hopi mask
Sedona, 1946
Later gelatin silver print

Katchina dolls on a dealer's roof and bought them up. They formed the basis of his large collection, with which he had himself photographed not much later. These wooden dolls of the Hopi and Zuni represented images of masked dancers that featured on ritual occasions. His 1950 lithograph of Masks, for example, shows – like numerous sculptures of the period – the influence of Indian models in both the subject matter and the geometrical style.

In 1946, Max Ernst won a Hollywood competition with his painting *The Temptation of St Anthony* (now in the Lehmbruck Museum, Duisburg), ahead of Salvador Dalí. With the prize-money he bought some land in Sedona (Arizona) and built a house for himself and his fourth wife, Dorothea Tanning. He decorated one of the outside walls

James Thrall Soby
Max Ernst with his Katchina collection on the terrace of the Guggenheim triplex
New York, 1942

THE YEARS IN THE USA 1941–1949

Dick Greening
Large frieze
Sedona, 1949

with a frieze made up of eight individual parts – animal heads, masks and a bird. Inspired by the geometrical pattern of the cracks in the wall, he added linear body shapes to the friezes in a second phase of work to make three figures. Their attitudes are reminiscent of the ritual dances of the Indians.

Not far from the house he did a figure group from cement, called Capricorn. For the internal structure he used bottles, iron bars and rings. The work is his largest sculpture, and he called it "his family". In its formal language, the work represents the sum of his previous figures. In terms of content, it presents his whole personal, mythological cosmos, which he had once set out to find.

Max Ernst
Masques/Masks, 1950
Lithograph

John Kasnetsis
Dorothea Tanning and Max Ernst with *Capricorn* cement sculpture
Sedona, 1948
Later gelatin silver print
Dorothea Tanning Bequest

*Switch on the searchlights
of the night's brain.*
Max Ernst

D-PAINTINGS Landscapes of Love

Jürgen Pech

On 25 August 2000, American artist Dorothea Tanning celebrated her 90th birthday. The city of Brühl used the occasion and this special year to put on two unusual, complementary exhibitions in the Max Ernst Kabinett, showing works by and for her. On the eve of her birthday, an exhibition of her drawings and books called "Birthday" opened to the public. On varnishing day, guests were able to write their congratulations, which were then faxed to Dorothea Tanning in New York. The pleasure and surprise were great – her previous solo show in Germany had been more than 35 years earlier. The public was delighted by the poetry of her works, whose hallucinatory clarity lies *somewhere between the inner eye and the other side of the door*, to quote the artist herself.

Max Ernst met Dorothea Tanning in New York in 1942. Four years later, on 24 October 1946, they celebrated a double wedding in Beverley Hills with Man Ray and Juliet Browner. The same year they moved to Sedona, Arizona, where they spent some years, initially in a modest wooden house they built themselves and to which a stone-built house was later added. They had visited Europe several times after the end of World War II, and in 1954 bought a modest farmhouse in Huismes in Touraine. Ten years later they moved to Seillans in the south of France, where in the late 1960s they built a house with two studios to plans by

Lee Miller
Max Ernst and Dorothea Tanning, Sedona, 1946
Later gelatin silver print

Dorothea. This and the flat in the Rue de Lille in Paris were where Max Ernst worked in his final years. This major artist of the 20th century died in Paris on 1 April 1976, on the eve of his 85th birthday.

During their 34 years together, Max Ernst dedicated a work to Dorothea every year; these are the "paintings for Dorothea" or D-paintings. It was this group of works, never shown in their entirety before, that was exhibited on Dorothea Tanning's 90th birthday in Brühl in 2000. As befitted the subject and the artist's delight in overturning conventions, D-shaped pretzels (dretzels) were served up at the opening of the exhibition in the Max Ernst Kabinett. The D initial can be found on every picture – the pleasure in seeing it is enhanced by the amusement of looking for it.

Mostly small-scale works, they are precious gems, landscapes of love. The works not only provide a focused view of the late years of the artist's oeuvre but also an overview of the variety of indirect techniques that he used – decalcomania, grattage, collage, object assemblage and frottage acting as sources of inspiration.

Five years later this unique suite of works, which reflects the many facets not only of Max Ernst's own oeuvre but also of the relationship between the artist couple, was acquired with the support of the Kreissparkasse in Cologne. It is a very personal ensemble, not least because Dorothea Tanning often used to rearrange the pictures on the walls of her apartment. It has now found a suitable home in the Max Ernst Museum in Brühl in a hanging that focuses on the personality of the artist.

Max Ernst
D 1943
Oil on wood
Permanent loan,
Kreissparkasse Köln

A subject that turns up many times in the D-paintings is illuminated night, the time of dreams. Thus the background of the late assemblage of wooden planks dated 1971 is deliberately kept dark. The relief-like fabric collage is a nocturne. Both the moon, for which the artist used an ornamental cloth reworked with white paint, and the letter, which he wrote with white chalk on the wooden forest on the right, shine out brightly from the darkness of night. The format of the work celebrated a particular occasion, since it was painted in the year of the couple's silver wedding.

Another night picture, *Les phases de la nuit* (D1946) from 25 years earlier, is conspicuous for its size. As here, the year of their wedding is singled out for special treat-

Max Ernst
D 1973
Chalk and collage from colour reproduction, drawing pins, textured wallpaper and ex-libris on card, Permanent loan, Kreissparkasse Köln

ment in the D-painting series. The 'phases of the night' title is poetically reminiscent of the time of sleep and dreams in an echo of the Surrealist evocation of dreams. The picture was based on the interpretation of decalcomania structures that, generated more or less randomly in the medium of oils, lent wings to the imagination and inspired the artist. The moon shines centrally over the standard-format landscape. Set against the orb of the moon is a bird hovering on outspread pinions. The swelling and ebbing shape of the wings and the movement of flight are to be interpreted quite generally as emblematic, since they visualise and vary a sequence – the phases of the night. The dotted sinusoidal curve in the foreground repeats and emphasises the sequence of movements like an oscillogram. Between the two crests and directly beneath the moon is the second radiant centre of the picture – an owl gleaming in warm tones as if from within. This beast, which can see in the night, is identified by the monogram visible in the feathers

Max Ernst
D 1971
Chalk, collage, doily,
mounted on wooden board
Permanent loan,
Kreissparkasse Köln

with Max Ernst himself. The line links him with a mask bearing the date on its forehead on the left and a combination of a house and another owl-like creature displaying the initial D on the right. The artist is bound here between the two poles of time and love. The night that Max Ernst presents here is not only the night of love but also the night of cognition.

Illumination is a feature that runs through the D-group like a leitmotif. In his landscapes of love, Max Ernst always depicts visions of the inward self, revelations based equally on experience and passion. Illuminations, nights of the full moon, gleaming yellow light reflections, sparkling polar

Max Ernst
Les phases de la nuit/
The Phases of the Night
(D 1946)
Oil on canvas, Permanent loan,
Kreissparkasse Köln

lights, brilliant rays of light and iridescent flashes represent the Surrealist sparks of poetry, but also the enchanted magic of love.

Denise Colomb
Max Ernst in La Hune bookshop, Paris, January 1950
Later gelatin silver print

MAX ERNST RETURNS TO FRANCE 1949–1976

Olaf Mextorf

> *My behaviour is much like my work:
> not harmonious in the manner
> of classical composers, or even of
> classic revolutionaries. Obstreperous,
> uneven, contradictory, it's unacceptable
> to specialists of art, culture, behaviour,
> logic and morality.*
>
> Max Ernst *Die Nacktheit der Frau ist weiser als die Lehre des Philosophen*

The crossing from New Orleans to Europe took three weeks in 1949. It was 'Schnabelmax's' first return to postwar Europe, and Dorothea Tanning went with him. It was only a provisional visit, a cautious rapprochement that would culminate in the couple finally moving to France in 1953.

In his 'biographical notes' Max Ernst describes the first period in Europe, talks about his work in a 'borrowed' studio in Paris and his visit to the *ruins of beloved Cologne with very mixed feelings*. Max Ernst *Wahrheitgewebe*

Although in artistic terms things were not looking too good for artists working in a Surrealist vein – abstraction had the front stage by then – as a returning exile Max Ernst was accorded a series of exhibitions and great admiration, but found few buyers.

Particularly important was the overview exhibition put on in Brühl in 1951 to celebrate his 60th birthday. His sister

Loni and her husband, Lothar Pretzell, organised the biggest Max Ernst exhibition to date at Schloss Augustusburg, with over 120 exhibits, and the exhibition went on tour to eight other German cities. Before this, there had been a major retrospective of his graphic works organised by the Paris bookshop La Hune. André Breton himself wrote the accompanying article, describing the importance of the graphic works for Max Ernst's work as a whole: *His graphic work spans a long time, and develops an ever greater emancipation of the eye.... Only a foolish gaze could accuse this art of dissecting the world whereas the contrary is in fact true – everything is striving to come together in a new structure.*

André Breton Max Ernst, *Livres, Illustrations, Gravures 1919–1949*

Under the slogans of continuity, expanded perception and an overall view, this exhibition was an early indication of the direction and emphasis of Max Ernst's further work. In hindsight, it is clear how much the graphic work – sometimes described as a kaleidoscope, sometimes as a constant experiment – moves to the foreground in the late oeuvre. The great Max Ernst connoisseur Werner Spies also notes the enormous richness of design that this genre allows: *The processes that Max Ernst took over, further developed or invented comprise more or less everything that can be done in graphic art in our century. And when he used them, in every case he went beyond traditional frontiers of graphic techniques. [...] When one surveys the henceforth increasing use of graphic prints, it turns out that these techniques, which permit of experimenting and entirely new effects, lead to ever different discoveries.* Werner Spies *Max Ernst – Graphik und Bücher*

When Max Ernst and Dorothea Tanning moved to France for good in 1953, his portofolio of graphic prints *Das Schnabelpaar* (Bird Couple) was published by Ernst Beyeler in Basle. It contains eight colour etchings, an embossed print and a poem by Max Ernst, impressively demonstrating his double talent as an artist and poet. Retrospect, transformation and a new beginning are the subjects of this work. Imbued with a basic optimism, it radiates a mysterious ebullience. Curving lines track ambivalent outlines that sometimes look like birds, at other times like humans. In parallel, finely structured colour surfaces bring variable picture volumes that directly express change and movement.

1954 was a turning point in Max Ernst's life, because in June he was awarded the grand prix for painting at the 27th Biennale in Venice. This award was just one of a whole series of further honours and titles to come that brought him international recognition and financial security. At last he was able to get his fragile plaster sculptures gradually

Max Ernst
Das Schnabelpaar/Bird Couple, sheet IV, 1953
Etching with aquatint

cast in bronze, and his sculpture gradually became more widely known.

In 1955, the couple moved to Huismes, a small place on the Loire south-west of Tours. Max Ernst continued work with undiminished energy. He produced etchings for Antonin Artaud's *Galapagos* (1955), some wonderful aquatints to accompany poems by Friedrich Hölderlin (1961), large-format lithographs such as *Hibou-Arlequin* (Owl Harlequin, 1955) and *La forêt à l'aube* (The Forest at Dawn, 1958) plus meticulously composed silkscreen prints such as *The Sea* (1957). He produced photo lithographs (*The Wooden Forest*, 1956)

Max Ernst
La forêt à l'aube / The Forest
at Dawn, 1958
Colour lithograph

and worked with the technique of offset printing (*documenta. Printed Graphics*, 1959). A first survey of his sculptural oeuvre in 1959 presented 20 sculptures, which were shown as part of a major retrospective in Paris.

When I find myself in a blind alley, which happens a lot, I've always got sculpture as a way out, because sculpture is even more fun than painting."

Max Ernst, in: Peter Schamoni, *Max Ernst – Maximiliana*

Just how liberating playing around with shapes could be, whether invented or found, is evident from works such as

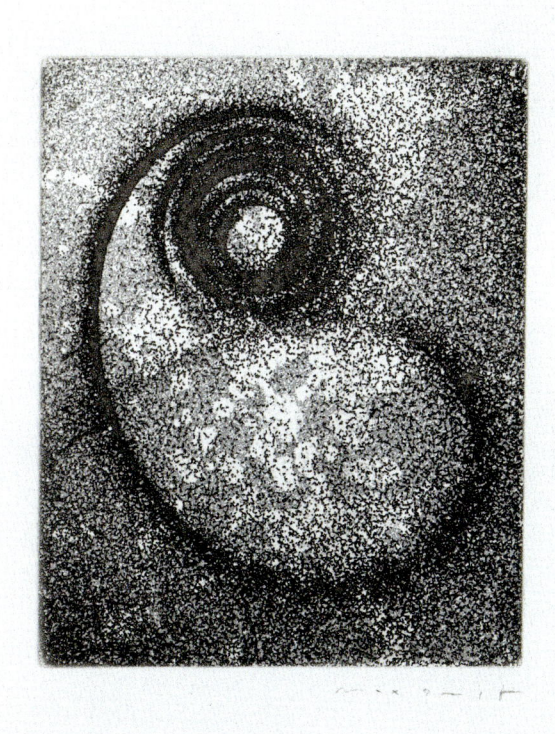

Max Ernst
Illustration for: Friedrich Hölderlin, *Poèmes,* sheet IV,
1961, Aquatint

Un microbe vu à travers un tempérament (Microbe Seen via a Constitution, 1964) and *Deux assistants* (Two Assistants, 1967). Sometimes it is the recognition of something familiar in an unfamiliar context, at other times sheer fun that prompts the viewer to go along with Max Ernst's interpreting eye.

In 1964, his worsening health forced Max Ernst to move south to Seillans in the vicinity of Cannes. In March the same year, his portfolio of *Maximiliana or the Illegal Exercise of Astronomy*, which for Werner Spies is the "summation of the illustrative works of Max Ernst". The *Maximiliana* is dedicated to the life and work of German astronomer and lithographer Ernst Wilhelm Leberecht Tempel (1821–1889), who in his

Max Ernst
Un microbe vu à travers
un tempérament /
A Microbe Seen through
a Constitution, 1964
Bronze
Permanent loan,
Kreissparkasse Köln

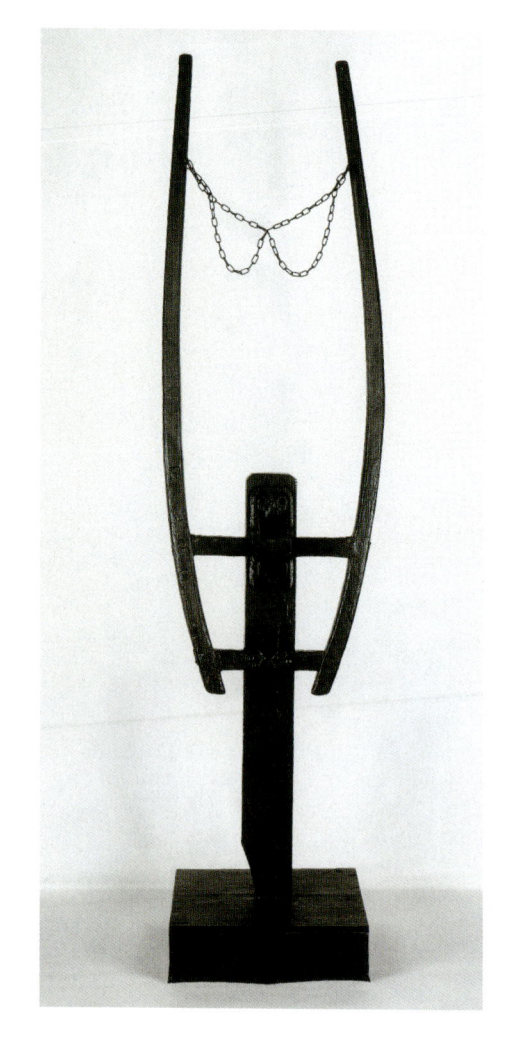

lifetime remained unrecognised despite discovering numerous stars and nebulae, including the planet Maximiliana of the title.

The extensive portfolio was produced in close collaboration with publisher, poet, printer and typographer Iliazd, who had done a lot of research into Tempel. It comprises 30 double-sided sheets with 34 coloured etchings and aquatints, printed drawings and vignettes. In addition there is a secret script invented by Max Ernst that runs throughout *Maximiliana* and was possibly inspired by the secret scripts of Red Indian medicine men. Iliazd took care of the typography of the texts and Georges Visat, a printer and friend of Max Ernst, enabled him to experiment with etching techniques. For many people, Maximiliana is one of the most important art books of the 20th century, while Max Ernst himself called it his finest book publication. The obvious pleasure in experimentation and the technical perfection

Max Ernst
**Deux assistants /
Two Assistants**, 1967
Bronze
Permanent loan,
Kreissparkasse Köln

of the semi-automatic etching techniques have frequently been called the ultimate in printed art.

The ideas expressed in *Maximiliana* continued to preoccupy him, as the artist's last works – numerous paintings, drawings and collages he produced between 1963 and 1974 – bear out.

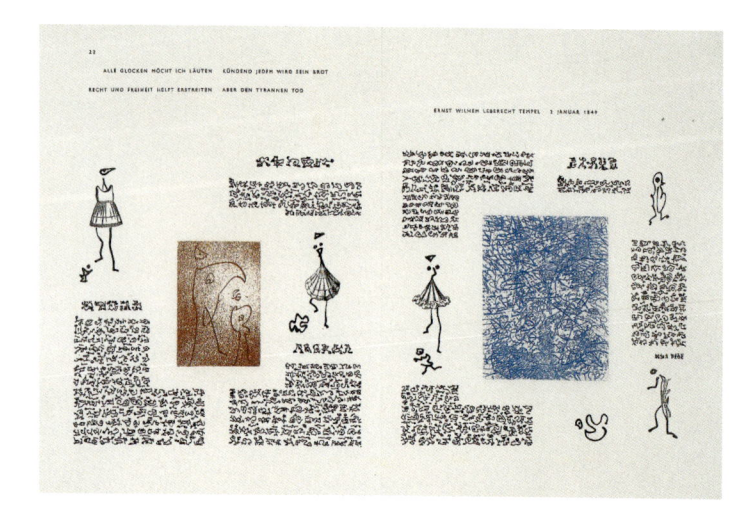

Maximiliana has a special significance for Brühl. After a rather prickly period in his relationship with his native town, it formed part of an extensive gift he made in 1969. The edition of this masterwork furnished with a long dedication became part of the foundation of the Max Ernst Kabinett that the town set up in honour of its artistic son in 1980. The municipal collection has steadily grown since then, and is a core part of the new Max Ernst Museum.

Max Ernst
Maximiliana, Sheet 22, 1964
Etching

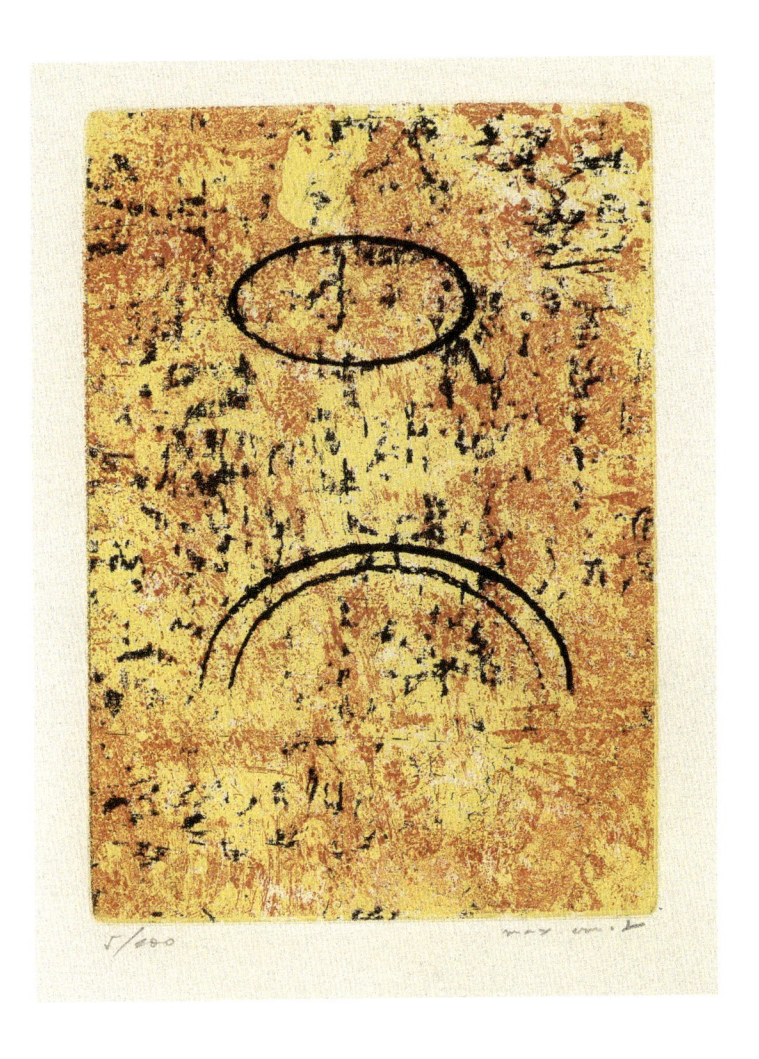

Max Ernst
Illustration for: Eddy Batache –
La Mysticité Charnelle de René Crevel/René Crevel's Carnal Mysticity, 1975
Etching and aquatint on paper

Max Ernst
L'œil sans yeux, la femme 100 têtes garde son secret/ The Eye Without Eyes, the Hundred-headed Woman Guards Her Secret, from: *La femme 100 têtes*, 1929
From a collage

WORKING METHODS AND TECHNIQUES

Katja Tallner

Many people are both fascinated and disconcerted by the works of Max Ernst. The mysterious landscapes and fantastic creatures he produced inevitably give rise to the question as to where this extraordinary artist drew his inspiration from. We are told that the sight of an empty canvas used to dismay him, even that he had a kind of virginity complex vis-à-vis the canvas [Werner Spies, *Max Ernst – Frottagen*]. The consequence was that he habitually sought ways to avoid applying paint directly with the brush or drawing with a pencil, and this prompted him to develop a lot of new techniques.

A further consequence was that chance became a key element of his work and largely replaced the controlled artistic approach governed by the conscious mind at the beginning of the work process. That was his way in to the visual worlds of the unconscious mind. He even went as far as to declare that *all 'active' control by reason, morality or aesthetic considerations were contrary to inspiration.* Max Ernst, *Was ist Surrealismus?*

This idea has its counterpart in the écriture automatique that Breton described in his Surrealist manifesto of 1924. Automatic writing was to be a 'liberating' process that would tend to keep the poet's or artist's habits and deliberate intentions out of the creative process.

By applying and developing various novel artistic techniques, Max Ernst undoubtedly extended the potential of his creative work quite considerably. Yet the uniqueness of his work consists principally in the selection and reinterpretation of the raw material.

COLLAGE

Ernst first experimented with collages in Cologne directly after the end of World War I, and it became his principal artistic technique, used even with traditional printing techniques such as lithography and etching.

A forerunner of collages were the *papiers collés* that Picasso and Braque employed when they first stuck real-world material on to their Cubist paintings. Collages as practised by Max Ernst bore little resemblance to these, however. *Si ce sont les plumes qui font le plumage, ce n'est pas la colle qui fait le collage (Feathers may go to make plumage, but glue doesn't make collages).*
Max Ernst Beyond Painting

Max Ernst understood collage *as an interpretation of the chance encounter between two distant realities.* Max Ernst Beyond Painting

Combining elements hitherto considered incompatible worked so convincingly for him because he went to great lengths to get rid of the visible joins between the parts. One way he did this was by reproduction, which concealed the different kinds of paper used. Another was by using homogeneous 19th-century wood engravings, which he cut up for his collage novels (1929–1934). In the works he did for *La femme 100 têtes* or *Une semaine de bonté*, the three-dimensionality of the source material was basically preserved but he changed the setting by adding individual objects or creatures.

Ernst applied the collage principle not only to painting and graphic works but to his sculptures as well. He started by replicating in plaster ordinary items such as car springs and milk bottles, which he used in *Capricorn*, so as to reconstitute them as imaginary creatures. The original functions of the raw materials are no longer recognisable in the new context.

BLOCK PRINTS

In 1919, Max Ernst came across the line blocks used for technical diagrams at the Hertz printing works in Cologne, where Dada publications *Bulletin D* and *Die Schammade* were printed. The blocks that inspired him he combined into montages, coloured them in and took pulls on the proofing machine. The result was then finished as drawing work. This technique produced a whole series for which Ernst constantly resorted to the same limited repertoire of set images, which he combined into ever new combinations. Such reuse of motifs he had already used was a feature of Max Ernst's entire oeuvre.

OVERPAINTINGS

The catalogue of the Kölner Lehrmittel-Anstalt teaching aids institute constituted a vital source of inspiration during his Dada time in Cologne. The wealth of teaching materials it offered for a wide range of subjects in the shape of diagrams, models etc. was the most important basis for overpaintings. He isolated individual elements by means of painting or drawing, concealed others or put the motifs into a new, striking context which obliterated the original meaning.

PHOTO COLLAGES / PHOTOGRAPHICS / PHOTOGRAMS

While he was in Cologne, Max Ernst developed his interest in photography, which provided source material for collages and also reproductions. In his photo collages he combined photographic materials with drawn elements. He might then add more collage elements to the photographic proofs or finish them off by means of drawing.

Max Ernst
The Punching Ball or The Immortality of Buonarroti, 1920
Collage on photograph and gouache, Chicago, Arnold H. Crane Collection

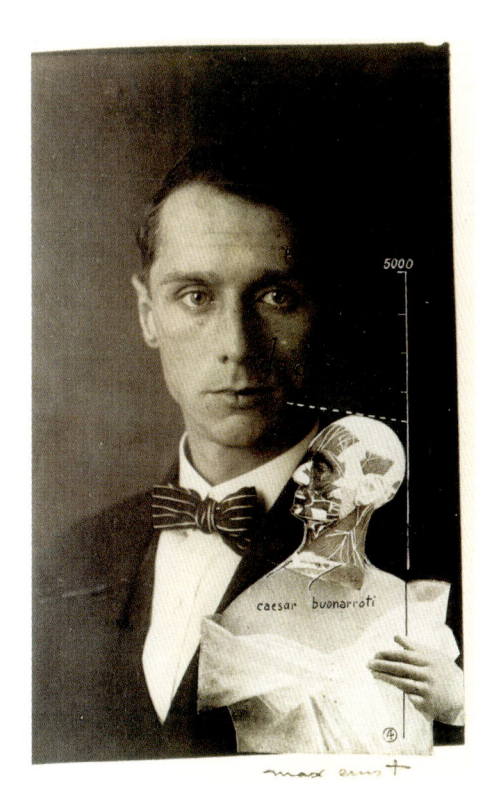

Max Ernst
Illustration for
René Crevel's
Mr. Knife and Miss Fork, 1931
Photogram

Photography is a good example of how Max Ernst pushed back the frontiers of 'classic' graphic techniques, since in this he surpassed even representatives of institutions such as the Bauhaus, who prided themselves on their progressiveness. His proposal to publish a photo edition (photographics) signed by him was considered provocative, since it did not respect the distinction between graphic works and originals. The works were thus despised as non-'artistic'.

However, by the time he did the illustrations for René Crevel's *Mr. Knife and Miss Fork* from 1931, which were based on photographic duplications of Ernst's frottages, sceptics must have been persuaded of the artistic opportunities that photographic techniques offered. Man Ray, for example, produced photograms from his frottage works. In this technique, the photographic paper is exposed to light through the frottages. The structures in the frottages screen out the light, thereby leaving white lines on a black background. Max Ernst constantly resorted to photomechanical repro procedures to reproduce his work and get rid of traces of his handiwork. It was a technique that raised a question mark over the hitherto prevailing concept of 'originals'.

FROTTAGE

Frottage is, technically speaking, just old-fashioned rubbing (as in brass-rubbing), where the pattern of a relief (or incised) surface is rubbed through on to a piece of paper placed on top of it. Max Ernst was using rubbings of printers' relief plates – wooden letters – to produce patterned supports already in 1919. But it was not until 1925 that he recognised the possibilities that the patterns on wooden boards, dried leaves, rope or even crumpled paper offered as well. 'Automatic' raw material of this kind could then

Victor Schamoni
Max Ernst at work on a frottage
Huismes, 1963
Later gelatin silver print
Dorothea Tanning Bequest

be combined into new arrangements. The 34 sheets of the *Histoire Naturelle* portfolio (published 1926) demonstrate most impressively what could be achieved artistically with rubbings.

GRATTAGE

Another technique based on random effects is grattage, which is really a variant of frottage. Paint is applied thickly to the canvas and then scraped or rubbed off so the layers below (boards, rope etc.) show through. Max Ernst discerned the makings of shapes such as the heads and bodies of birds in the patterns thus produced, which he then worked up by extending outlines and adding details.

DECALCOMANIA

The first to use decalcomania as an artistic technique was Oscar Dominguez in 1936. A detailed description of the method is given in the *Dictionnaire abrégé du Surréalisme* (1938): *Spread occasionally diluted black gouache with a thick brush on smooth white paper, and place a similar sheet on top of it, pressing it lightly,*

Max Ernst
D 1943
Oil on wood, Permanent loan, Kreissparkasse Köln

then lift the second sheet off. Decalcomania derives from letterpress printing on a printing press. In both cases, chance plays an important part in the genesis of new patterns. Max Ernst worked not with gouache but diluted oils. Depending on the shapes that the decalcomania produced (reminiscent of organic or mineral structures), he worked them up with the brush into landscapes, figures or monsters.

OSCILLATION

Typical of works in this technique are curved lines such as are to be seen in the painting Surrealism and Painting (1942). Here, Max Ernst developed a novel method of applying paint – he filled a can with a hole in it with paint and swung it over the support on the end of a line, so that paint dripped out on to the canvas in a controlled way. Indirectly, this was an influential innovation in that American artist Jackson Pollock later developed oscillation into 'dripping' and 'action painting'.

BIOGRAPHY

Unknown
Max at five with his older sister Maria
Brühl, 1896
Private collection

Unknown
Max Ernst as a schoolboy
Brühl, 1909
Vintage, silver bromide print

1891	Born in Brühl near Cologne on 2 April, the son of deaf-mute teacher and painter Philipp Ernst and his wife, Luise, née Kopp, of Schloss Straße 21, Brühl
1910–14	Studies Philology, Philosophy, Psychology and Art History at the University of Bonn
1911	Becomes friends with August Macke
1913	Art and theatre critic for the *Bonner Volksmund* paper
	Takes part in the exhibition of Rhineland Expressionists at Cohen's Art and Bookshop in Bonn
	Meets Guillaume Apollinaire and Robert Delaunay at August Macke's house

BIOGRAPHY

1914	Acquaintance with Hans Arp
1914–18	Military service during World War I
1916	Home leave from the front
	First solo exhibition at the Sturm gallery in Berlin
1918	Marries art historian Luise Straus
	Returns to Cologne
1919	Visits Paul Klee
	Sees works of de Chirico for the first time
	Takes part in Dada activities in Cologne
1920	Dada *Early Spring* exhibition in Winter's Brewery in Cologne
	Birth of his son Ulrich (Jimmy)
1921	First exhibition in Paris
	Meets Tristan Tzara, André Breton, Hans Arp and Sophie Taeuber in Tarrenz (Tyrol): joint manifesto 'Dada au Grand Air – the War of Singers in Tyrol'
	Becomes acquainted with Paul Eluard and his wife, Gala, in Cologne
1922	Moves to Paris; moves in with Paul and Gala Eluard in Saint-Brice
1923	Decorates the Eluard house in Eaubonne with murals

Unknown
Hans Arp, Tristan Tzara and Max Ernst in the garden of the Sonne Inn in Tarrenz, near Imst
August/September 1921
Rolandseck, Stiftung Hans Arp und Sophie Taeuber-Arp

Max Ernst
Self-Portrait, c. 1938
Frottage
Chalk on photograph
Sprengel Museum, Hanover
On loan from the Niedersächsische Sparkassenstiftung

1924	Spends several months in Indochina
1925	Discovers the technique of frottage
1926	Divorces Luise Straus
	Portfolio of graphic prints: *Histoire Naturelle*
1927	Marries Marie-Berthe Aurenche, sister of film director Jean Aurenche
1929	First collage novel *La femme 100 têtes*
1930	Film role in Luis Buñuel's *L'Age d'Or*
1932	First solo exhibition at the Julien Levy Gallery, New York
1934	Writes 'Was ist Surrealismus?' as preface to a Surrealist exhibition at the Kunsthaus Zürich
1935	Stays with Alberto Giacometti in Maloja, Switzerland
1937	Divorces Marie-Berthe Aurenche
	Max Ernst denounced by the Nazis, with two pictures in the 'Degenerate Art' exhibition in Munich
1938	Withdraws from the Surrealist group and moves to Saint-Martin d'Ardèche (N of Avignon) with painter Leonora Carrington

Victor Schamoni
Max Ernst's house in Saint-Martin d'Ardèche, 1990
Private collection

Lee Miller
Double portrait of Dorothea Tanning and Max Ernst
Sedona, early August 1946

1939–40	Interned several times in French camps after the outbreak of war
	Does his first works in the decalcomania technique invented by Oscar Dominguez
1941	Emigrates to the USA
	Marries art collector Peggy Guggenheim
1943	Divorces Peggy Guggenheim
1944	Works on plaster sculptures in Great River on Long Island; The King Playing with the Queen is shown in the 'The Imagery of Chess' group exhibition at the Julien Levy Gallery in New York
1946	Marries painter Dorothea Tanning (double wedding with Man Ray and Juliet Browner) and moves to Sedona (Arizona)
1948	Acquires American citizenship; produces *Capricorn*
1950	Retrospective of graphic works at La Hune bookshop in Paris
1951	First major retrospective at Schloss Augustusburg in Brühl
1953	Returns to Paris; travels around Germany (Cologne, Brühl, Bonn, Heidelberg)
	First exhibition at the Spiegel gallery in Cologne

John Kasnetsis
Dorothea Tanning and Max Ernst with the *Capricorn* cement sculpture, Sedona, 1948
Later gelatin silver print
Dorothea Tanning Bequest

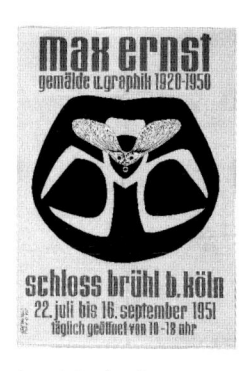

Joseph Fassbender
(from a collage by Max Ernst)
Poster for Max Ernst exhibition at Schloss Augustusburg
Brühl, 1951

1954	Wins grand prix for painting at the 27th Biennale in Venice
1955	Moves to Huismes near Chinon (SW of Tours)
1958	Acquires French citizenship
1964	Settles with Dorothea Tanning in Seillans in the south of France; publishes *Maximiliana* (together with Iliazd)
1966	Turns down freedom of the town of Brühl
	Peter Schamoni shoots the *Illegal Exercise of Astronomy*
	Fountain in Amboise dedicated
1971	Fountain in Brühl dedicated

Victor Schamoni
Max Ernst in his studio
Huismes 1963
1970s reprint
Private collection

BIOGRAPHY

1971	Honorary doctorate of the University of Bonn
1975	In Paris
1976	Max Ernst dies in his flat in Paris on the eve of his 85th birthday.

Edward Quinn
Max Ernst in front of the painting *Here are Three Earthquakes*
Seillans, autumn 1966
Reprint

*Close your physical eye,
that you may see your image
first in your mind's eye.*
C. D. Friedrich

Bill Brandt
Max Ernst's left eye
Paris, 1965, Vintage after
Gelatin silver print

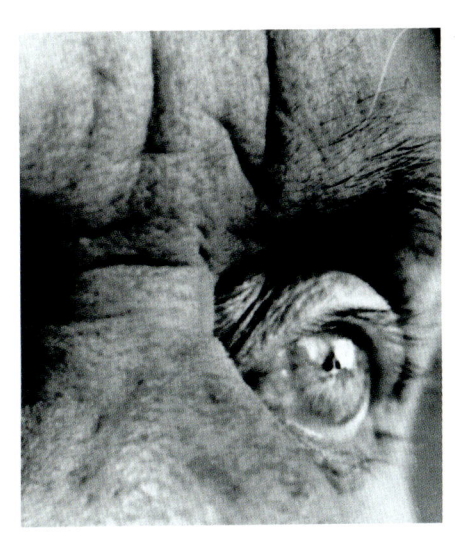

Bibliography

Max Ernst, *Was ist Surrealismus?* (What is Surrealism?), exhib. cat. (Kunsthaus), Zurich 1934 [reprinted in: Metken 1976, pp. 323–25]
Max Ernst, *Au delà de la peinture* in: *Cahiers d'Art* XI, no. 6/7, 1936, pp. 149–84. Engl. version: Beyond Painting 1948
Max Ernst, *Einiges aus Max Ernsts Jugend von ihm selbst erzählt* (Some Things about Max Ernst's Youth, Told by Himself), 1942
Max Ernst, *Die Nacktheit der Frau ist weiser als die Lehre der Philosophen* (The Nakedness of Woman is Wiser than the Doctrine of Philosophers), 1962
Max Ernst, *Biographische Notizen. Wahrheitgewebe und Lügengewebe* (Biographical Notes. Web of Truth and Lies), in: Max Ernst, exhib. cat. (Wallraf-Richartz Museum), Cologne 1963

Peter Barth, *Johanna Ey und ihr Künstlerkreis* (Johanna Ey and Her Artist Friends), exhib. cat. (Galerie Remmert und Barth, Düsseldorf), Düsseldorf 1984
Ulrich Bischoff, *Max Ernst 1891–1976. Jenseits der Malerei* (Beyond Painting), Cologne 1987
André Breton, *Max Ernst, livres, illustrations, gravures, 1919–1949*, 1950
Dietmar Elger/Uta Grosenick (eds.), *Dadaismus*, Cologne etc. 2004
Jimmy Ernst, *Nicht gerade ein Stilleben. Erinnerungen an meinen Vater Max Ernst* (son's memoirs of his father), Cologne 1985
Alfred M. Fischer/Gabriele Lohberg, *Max Ernst: Druckgraphische Werke und illustrierte Bücher* (Printed Graphics and Illustrated Books), exhib. cat. (Museum Ludwig, Cologne/Städtische Galerie, Linz), Cologne 1990. Particularly relevant: Gabriele Lohberg, 'Maximiliana. Über die legale Ausübung der Buchkunst' and Winfried Konnertz, 'Es ist mir nicht gegeben, den Spezialisten zu gefallen'. (about Max Ernst's graphic works)
Lothar Fischer, *Max Ernst in Selbstzeugnissen und Bilddokumenten* (Max Ernst seen through his writings and pictures), Reinbek 1969
Silke Margarete Giersch, *Das Frühwerk von Max Ernst* (on the early work, 1906/7–1919). *Max Ernst vor der Collage* (Max Ernst before Collages, dissertation (typescript), FU Berlin 1998
Wulf Herzogenrath (ed.), *Max Ernst in Köln. Die rheinische Kunstszene bis 1922* (Max Ernst in Cologne. The Rhineland Art Scene up to 1922), exhib. cat. (Kunstverein), Cologne 1980
Sidney Janis, *Abstract and Surrealist Art in America,* New York 1944
Katsinam. Figuren der Pueblo-Indianer Nordamerikas aus der Studiensammlung Horst Antes (Horst Antes Collection of Katchina figures), ed. Horst Antes, exhib. cat. (Ethnological Collection, Lübeck), Lübeck 2000

BIBLIOGRAPHY

Winfried Konnertz, *Max Ernst. Zeichnungen, Aquarelle, Übermalungen, Frottagen* (drawings, watercolours, overpaintings, frottages), Cologne 1980

Max Ernst. Œuvre-Katalog (Catalogue of Works), vol. 1, *Das graphische Werk* (The Graphic Works), Helmut R. Leppien et al., vols. 2–6, *Werke* (Works) *1906–1925; 1925–1929; 1929–1938; 1939–1953; 1954–1963*, Werner Spies, Sigrid Metken, Günter Metken, (Menil Foundation, Houston), Cologne 1975–98

Max Ernst und Bonn. Student, Kritiker, Rheinischer Expressionist (Max Ernst and Bonn. Student, Critic and Rhineland Expressionist), ed. Verein August Macke Haus e. V. (Schriftenreihe Verein August Macke Haus, Bonn, no. 13), Bonn 1994

Max Ernst – Fotografische Porträts und Dokumente (on the photographic portraits and documents, ed. Stadt Brühl, exhib. cat. (Town Hall, Brühl), Brühl 1991

Max Ernst: Skulpturen, Häuser, Landschaften (Max Ernst: Sculptures, Houses, Landscapes), exhib. cat. (Centre National d'Art et de Culture Georges Pompidou, Paris/Kunstsammlung Nordrhein-Westfalen, Düsseldorf), Cologne 1998

Max Ernst – Graphische Welten. Die Sammlung Schneppenheim (graphic works in the Schneppenheim Collection), ed. Kreissparkasse Köln, Cologne 2003

Günter Metken (ed.), *Als die Surrealisten noch recht hatten* (When the Surrealists were Still Right), Stuttgart 1976

Jürgen Pech, *Max Ernst – Skulpturen*, exhib. cat. (Stadtgalerie, Klagenfurt), Klagenfurt 1997

Sabine Rewald, Werner Spies (eds.), *Max Ernst. A Retrospektive*, exhib. cat. (The Metropolitan Museum of Art, New York), New York 2005

Peter Schamoni, *Max Ernst – Maximiliana. Die widerrechtliche Ausübung der Astronomie*, Munich 1974

Uwe M. Schneede, *Max Ernst*, Stuttgart 1972

Werner Spies, *Max Ernst – Collagen. Inventar und Widerspruch* (Collages. Inventory and Contradiction), Cologne 1974

Werner Spies (ed.), *Max Ernst Retrospektive 1979*, exhib. cat. (Haus der Kunst, Munich), Munich 1979

Werner Spies, *Max Ernst, Loplop. Die Selbstdarstellung des Künstlers* (Max Ernst, Loplop. The Self-Representation of the Artist), Munich 1982

Werner Spies, *Max Ernst – Frottagen*, Stuttgart ^{2}1986

Werner Spies, *Max Ernst – Graphik und Bücher*, Lufthansa Collection, ed. Deutsche Lufthansa AG, exhib. cat. (Württembergischer Kunstverein, Stuttgart), Stuttgart 1991

Werner Spies (ed.), *Max Ernst Retrospektive zum 100. Geburtstag*, (retrospective to mark the 100th anniversary of Max Ernst's birth), exhibit. cat. (Tate Gallery, London/Staatsgalerie, Stuttgart/Kunstsammlung Nordrhein-Westfalen, Düsseldorf), Munich 1991

Dorothea Tanning, *Birthday: Lebenserinnerungen* (memoirs), Cologne 1990

Vom Dadamax zum Grüngürtel. Köln in den 20er Jahren (Cologne in the 1920s), exhib. cat. (Kunstverein, Cologne), Cologne 1975

C. Sylvia Weber (ed.), *Max Ernst in der Sammlung Würth: Graphik, Bücher und Bilder* (Max Ernst in the Würth Collection: Graphics, Books and Paintings), Künzelsau 2000

Max Ernst Museum, 2004
South view
Photo: Rainer Mader

Information about the Museum

www.maxernstmuseum.de

CURATOR OF THE FOUNDING EXHIBITION
(4 Sept. 2005 – 5 March 2006)
Werner Spies

CURATOR OF THE REVOLVING EXHIBITION
(4 Sept. 2005 – probably 4 Sept. 2006)
Peter Schamoni

ARCHITECTURE *Architekturgemeinschaft van den Valentyn*:
Thomas van den Valentyn Architektur
Gloria Amling, Project partner;
smo Architektur: S. Mohammad Oreyzi

CONSTRUCTION *Harms Partner GbR Bauingenieure*:
Otto Reinebeck

ADDRESS *Max Ernst Museum*
Comesstraße 42
D-50321 Brühl

OPENING HOURS *Tuesday to Sunday* 11 am – 6 am
1st Thursday of the month 11 am – 9 am
Closed Mondays

MUSEUM CLOSED ON Easter Monday, 1 May, Whit Monday,
Good Friday, 24–25 December,
31 December, 1 January

Information about guided group visits,
bookings and advice: Kulturinfo Rheinland
Tel. 018 05 - 74 34 65 263
(12ct./min.)

Photo Credits

It has not been possible to trace the legal owners of all the works. Legitimate claims will, of course, be settled within the framework of conventional agreements.

Bergheim, Manfred J. Junggeburth cover
Berlin, Archiv Galerie Brusberg 30
Bonn, Kurt Bingler 37
Brühl, Max Ernst Museum (photo: Harald Blondiau)
    18 bottom, 19–23, 27, 33–35, 43 bottom, 55–57,
    60–62, 66, 70 bottom, 74 top
Brühl, Max Ernst Museum, on permanent loan from
    the Kreissparkasse Köln (photo: Harald Blondiau)
    36, 47–51, 58–59, 68
Brühl, Max Ernst Museum, on permanent loan from the
    Deutsche Bank (Photograph: Harald Blondiau) 2/3
Chicago, Arnold H. Crane Collection 65
Chiddingly/East Sussex, Lee Miller Archives 41, 46,
    73 top
Cologne, Van den Valentyn (photo: Rainer Mader)
    10, 12–16, 78
Hanover, Sprengel Museum, on loan from the Niedersächsische Sparkassenstiftung 71 bottom
London, Noya Brandt 75 bottom
London, Lord Snowdon/Camera Press/Picture Press 6
Munich, Getty Images 38
Munich, Peter Schamoni Film 67, 72, 74 bottom
Paris, Ministère de la Culture de France 52
Paris, Werner Spies 43 top
Private collection 17, 18 top, 29, 40, 42, 44, 70 top,
    73 bottom, 75 top
Rolandseck, Stiftung Hans Arp und Sophie Taeuber-Arp
    26, 71 top